PADRE PIO
MASS PRAYER BOOK

D1320563

by

Fr. Paul Trinchard, S.T.L.

Praying the Canonized Latin Rite
Liturgy as Salutary Oblation

Published by

MAETA
METAIRIE LOUISIANA

Published by MAETA

Printed in the United States of America

Library of Congress Control Number
2002093203

ISBN 1-889168-25-4

MAETA
P.O. BOX 6012
METAIRIE LA 70009-6012

THE CRUCIFIX

The Crucifix [bronze plaque by J.S. Sargent] **shows the Redemption of mankind...as envisaged...by Jesus on the Cross...**[Sargent] **confronts...**[us with]**...an amazing unity of thought and presentation...He shows us how things stand now and forever between us and Almighty God, and proclaims in sculptured silence the secret mysteries of the Mass.**

In the midst, is the figure of the Son of Man, who alone is...Son of God; and the race of...men is gathered around Him, whom their sins have crucified...[as represented by Adam and Eve or the Elect of mankind].

[Christ] is dead...and yet, alive: dead, but not...helpless or hanging from the Cross. He rises above His guilty kindred, erect, without support, upheld by some hidden

Cover: The cover picture of a bronze plaque by J. S. Sargent is from a National Gallery photo (London).

and mysterious vitality other than the mere human life that has passed away. He is nailed ...but it is not the nails that hold those arms stretched straight and level...[nor] the nail that supports the transfixed feet. The benignant and quiet majesty of the figure, the poise, and super-human bearing, the attitude of blessing in the outspread arms and the hands turned towards us, force us to notice Who it is that men have crucified: not man only, but God [made man].

Crouching beneath the right arm is Adam, awestruck and bewildered, and beneath the left is Eve whose head is bowed and face hid in shame and grief. Each holds a cup to catch the sacred blood. In these two, the sinning parents of us all...present under the Cross of Jesus Christ.

Lifted up from the earth, He draws all men to Himself and

gathers His guilty kindred close into his atoning sacrifice. "Drink, He seems to say...this precious Blood which your sins have shed. In it is life—My Life, obedient, guiltless and one with God. I bequeath you all I have, my life-blood, my very self..I make you partakers of my Godhead, and My Eternal Life."

The terms of this inheritance are...writ large in that band...passing over the shoulders of the High Priest and Victim across the shoulders of Adam and Eve, binding all mankind to Jesus in one huge Stole of Sacrifice. It is the token of [the Elects'] priesthood...for each Christian life must be spent united to [Christ Crucified]...in one multitudinous self-surrender and oblation to the will and purposes of God.

The stole cannot be loosened without destroying the meaning....essential to the doctrine which is re-stated and emphasized in the symbol of the Pelican, in the writhing serpent whose head is transfixed by the nail that pierces the feet of Christ and again without symbol in the ancient text:

Factus Homo Factor Hominis Factique: Redemptor Corporeus Redimo Corpora Corda Deus.

("Maker and Redeemer of mankind, I, God, becoming man, redeem in My flesh, the bodies and the souls of men.")

From the book, *Mysteries of the Mass in Reasoned Prayers,* by Fr. W. Roche, S.J.

"For the Victim is one and the same, the same now offering by the ministry of priests, who once offered Himself on the Cross, the manner of offering alone being different." In other words, although there are as many Sacrifices as there are Mass Offertories, at the same time, there does exist a real oneness between them and the One Offering and Offered on the Cross, as well as, at the Last Supper and eternally, in Heaven.

Council of Trent, Sess. 22

The Canonized Mass Liturgy As Salutary Oblation

The Canon of the Latin Mass contains the seriously binding "words of the Mass," which must be said by every Latin Rite priest. These Mass prayers begin with the *"Suscipe sancte Pater..."* and conclude with the *"Per Ipsum..."*

The Catholic Church has always held and taught that to come into Christ-priest's Mass *after* he begins these prayers or leave before he finishes them (and receives Holy Communion) voids the fulfilment of one's Mass attendance obligation. The *sensus et praxis fidelium* has spoken dogmatically and irreversibly!

What has come to be misleadingly labeled as the *Canon* [beginning with *"Te igitur..."* is really *Canon actionis* according to Fr. Jungmann (*Mass of the Roman Rite,* Benzinger Brothers, 1953, Vol. 2, p. 10).] *"Actio..."* defined the section [beginning with *"Te igitur..."*] as sacred activity; *"incipit canon actionis*–Here begins the Canon of the [salutary] action...(Ibid. P. 102)." Jungmann (quoting Annalar) confirms our "precise definition" of *Canon*: "The subdeacon takes the paten *medio canone, id est cum dicitur 'Te igitur'"* (Ibid., p. 103). The *"Te igitur"* comes in the middle of the *general* Canon (in fact, it is number ten of the twenty-one Canonized Latin Mass prayers).

What is this "salutary oblation" to which every canonized Mass prayer refers? When capitalized, the words "Salutary" and Oblation refer to Christ's Oblation (e.g. "Salutary Oblation"). When referring to "our" oblation in Christ, they will not be capitalized. The definitions or nuances of "salutary oblation" which occur within the Canonized Latin Mass Liturgy are as follows:

● Christ's Last Supper Oblation;

● Christ's Calvary Oblation (as once and forever actualizing the *Salutary Will realized* at the Last Supper);

● the Elect's Christ-ed oblations;

● this "here and now" Mass Oblation (as done by the priest in prayer/ritual);

● the Elects' oblation into Christ's Oblation;

● each Elect one actualizing Christ's Oblation in his life;

● and, the *"in primis"* Mass at the Last Supper; and/or, each Mass on earth; and/or the eternal Mass, Heaven.

The purpose of this booklet is to bring us to pray the Canonized Mass Prayers of the Latin Rite (from *"Suscipe Sancte Pater...* to *"Per Ipsum, cum Ipso et in Ipso...)* in light of their expressing or implying Salutary Oblation (as previously defined).

St. Padre Pio, priest-saint of the Canonized Mass, help restore the Canonized Mass among us.

St. Padre Pio, pray for us!

DEDICATION

Francisco Forgione, our beloved and sainted Padre Pio, took Pio as his religious name in honor of Pope Saint Pius V, who dogmatically canonized the Latin Mass text, the only Mass Padre Pio ever said. He prayed this Mass with such priestly fervor that he was the first and (to date) the only priest to manifest in his own body, the Mass he was privileged to celebrate.

Understanding the Mass as Christ's Oblation brings the realization that Christ's Salutary Oblation requires a response from the Elect. Padre Pio forever became who he is through his Mass oblation. His Mass oblation was prayed and lived: in, through and unto Christ's Oblation.

This prayerbook, dedicated to Padre Pio, hopes to teach Catholics to live the Mass: each Catholic offering the daily sufferings, joys and happenings of his own life through, in and into Christ's Holy Sacrifice of Calvary in order to become part of Christ's Memory, as expressed by Christ at His Last Supper and Testament. Therefore, it is only fitting to have this Mass prayerbook named after Padre Pio, the only stigmatist priest-saint of the Canonized Mass.

Fr. Paul Trinchard

"THE MASS"
THE LITURGY of the WORD

There exists two major parts of Divine Liturgy (often referred to as "the Mass"): the Liturgy of the Word (the Mass of the Catechumens) and the Liturgy of the Eucharist (which liturgy, *de facto*, constitutes "the Mass"). The Mass, therefore, (Mass of the Faithful) should be attended and prayed only by properly disposed baptized Catholics.

The Liturgy of the Word begins with a confession of sins and a plea for God's mercy (Psalm 42 and the Confiteor) and ends with the Creed, when said.

IN NOMINE PATRIS, *et Filii ✠ et Spiritus Sancti. Amen.*

PSALM 42
Judica me, Deus, et discerne causam meam de gente non sancta: ab homine iniquo, et doloso erue me.
S. Quia tu es Deus fortitudo mea quare me repulisti, et quare tristis incedo, dum affligit me inimicus?

"THE MASS"
THE LITURGY OF THE WORD

IN THE NAME of the Father and of the Son and of the Holy Ghost. Amen.

PSALM 42

O GOD, champion my cause against faithless people. Rescue me from evil and deceitful men. Indeed, Thou art my God, my only strength, my only hope.

Why does loneliness envelope me? Why does the enemy's oppression sadden me? Comfort me, O God, with Thy truth.

Lead me into Thy light. Bring me unto Thy holy mountain, the altar of Thy Holy Sacrifice and the altar of Thy abiding presence.

Emitte lucem tuam, et veritatis tuam: ipsa me deduxerunt, et adduxerunt in montem sanctum tuum et in tabernacula tua. Et introibo ad altare Dei: ad Deum qui laetificat juventutem meam.

S. *Confitebor tibi in cithara, Deus, Deus meus: Quare tristis es anima mea, et quare conturbas me?*

P. *Spera in Deo, quoniam adhuc confitebor illi: salutare vultus mei, et Deus meus.*
S. *Gloria Patri, et Filio et Spiritui Sancto.*

P. *Sicut erat in principio, et nunc, et semper: et in saecula saeculorum. Amen.*
S. *Introibo ad altare Dei.*

P. *Ad Deum qui laetificat juventutem meam.*
S. *Adjutorium nostrum* ✠ *in nomine Domini.*
P. *Qui fecit coelum et terram.*

✠

Here in Thy sanctuary, here on Thine altar dost Thou dwell, my God, my life and my joy. Here will I adore Thee, O God, my God.

Why then, art thou still downcast, O my soul? Hope in God. Adore Him.

Come unto His holy altar. Here, He is ever present to bestow grace and mercy.

Glory be to the Father, and to the Son and to the Holy Ghost, as it was in the beginning, is now and ever shall be, world without end. Amen.

O LORD, have mercy on me, a sinner!

✠

CONFITEOR

After Christ-priest prays the Confiteor, the Server prays:

Confiteor Deo omnipotenti, beatae Mariae semper Virgini, beato Michaeli Archangelo, beato Joanni Baptistae, sanctis Apostolis Petro et Paulo, omnibus Sanctis, et tibi Pater: quia peccavi nimis cogitatione, verbo et opere: (strike breast thrice) *mea culpa, mea culpa, mea maxima culpa. Ideo precor beatam Mariam semper Virginem, beatum Michaelem Archangelum, beatum Joannem Baptistam, sanctos Apostolos Petrum et Paulum, omnes Sanctos, et te, Pater, orare pro me ad Dominum Deum nostrum. Misereatur vestri omnipotens Deus, et dimissis peccatis vestris, perducat vos ad vitam aeternam.*

S. Amen.

P. Indulgentiam ✠ *absolutionem, et remissionem peccatorum nostrorum tribuat nobis omnipotens, et misericors Dominus.*
S. Amen.

CONFITEOR

I CONFESS to Almighty God, to Blessed Mary ever Virgin, to Blessed Michael the Archangel, to Blessed John the Baptist, to the Holy Apostles Peter and Paul, to all the Saints and to you, Father, that I have sinned exceedingly in thought, word and deed, (strike breast 3 times) **through my fault, through my fault, through my most grievous fault. Therefore, I beseech Blessed Mary ever Virgin, Blessed Michael the Archangel, Blessed John the Baptist, the Holy Apostles Peter and Paul, all the saints, and you, Father, to pray to the Lord our God for me.**

May Almighty God forgive us our sins and grant us salvation from Hell unto Heaven. O Lord, as Thou freely bestoweth salvation, only thus is salvation given. Hear our one and only prayer: O Lord, we pray for salvation.

Deus, tu conversus vivificabis nos.
S. Et plebs tua laetabitur in te.
Ostende nobis Domine, miseicordiam tuam.
S. Et salutare tuum da nobis.
Domine, exaudi orationem meam.
S. Et clamor meus ad te veniat.
Dominus vobiscum. S. Et cum spiritu tuo. P. Oremus.

Aufer a nobis, quaesumus, Domine, iniquitates nostras: Ut ad Sancta sanctorum puris mereamur mentibus introire. Per Christum Dominum nostrum. Amen.
Oramus te, Domine, per merita Sanctorum tuorum, quorum reliquiae hic sunt, et omnium Sanctorum: ut indulgere digneris omnia peccata mea. Amen.

P. Kyrie eleison. S. Kyrie eleison. P. Kyrie eleison.
S.Christe eleison. P. Christe eleison. S.Christe eleison.
P. Kyrie eleison. S. Kyrie eleison. P. Kyrie eleison.

Gloria in excelsis Deo. Et in terra pax hominibus bonae voluntatis. Laudamus te. Benedicimus te. Adoramus te. Glorificamus te. Gratias agimus tibi propter magnam gloriam tuam. Domine Dues, Rex coelestis, Deus Pater omnipotens. Domine Fili unigenite Jesu Christe. Domine Deus, Agnus Dei, Filius Patris. Qui tollis peccata mundi, miserere nobis. Qui tollis peccata mundi, suscipe deprecationem nostram. Qui sedes ad dexteram Patris, miserere nobis. Quoniam tu solus Sanctus. Tu solus Dominus. Tu solus Altissimus, Jesu Christe. Cum Sancto Spiritu ✠ in gloria Dei Patris. Amen.

P. Dominus vobiscum. S. Et cum spiritu tuo. P. Oremus.

Take away from us our sins, O Lord, we beseech Thee, that we may enter with pure minds into the Holy of Holies. Through Christ our Lord. Amen.

We beseech Thee, O Lord, by the merits of Thy saints whose relics lie here, and of all the saints: deign in Thy mercy to pardon me all my sins. Amen.

Lord have mercy.   Lord have mercy. Lord have mercy. Christ have mercy.Christ have mercy.Christ have mercy. Lord have mercy. Lord have mercy. Lord have mercy.

Glory to God in the highest. And on earth peace to men of good will. We praise Thee. We bless Thee. We adore Thee. We glorify Thee. We give Thee thanks for Thy great glory. O Lord God, heavenly King, God the Father Almighty. O Lord Jesus Christ, the Only-begotten Son. O Lord God, Lamb of God, Son of the Father Who takest away the sins of the world, have mercy on us. Who takest away the sins of the world, receive our prayer. Who sittest at the right hand of the Father, have mercy on us. For Thou alone art holy. Thou alone art the Lord. Thou alone, O Jesus Christ, art most high. Together with the Holy Ghost ✠ in the glory of God the Father. Amen.

EPISTLE

Having confessed our guilt before God and having pled for His mercy and help, we listen to God's Word.

Christ-priest prays:

MUNDA cor meum, ac labia mea, omnipotens Deus, qui labia Isaiae prophetae calculo mundasti ignito: ita me tua grata miseratione dignare mundare, ut sanctum Evangelium tuum digne valeam nuntiare. Per Christum Dominum nostrum. Amen.

Jube, Domine benedicere.
Dominus sit in corde meo et in labiis meis: ut digne et competenter annuntiem Evangelium suum. Amen.

GOSPEL

Dominus vobiscum.   *S. Et cum spiritu tuo.*
✠*Sequentia (vel Initium) sancti Evangeli secundum N.*   *S. Gloria tibi, Domine.*
Stand for the Gospel.

After the Gospel, Christ-priest gives a sermon. At this part of his Mass, he acts as Christ to his flock.

EPISTLE

Having confessed our guilt before God and having pled for His mercy and help, we listen to God's Word.

We pray:

CLEANSE my heart and mind, and direct my will, O Almighty God, Who cleansed the lips of the prophet Isaias with a burning coal. In Thy gracious mercy, deign so to purify me that I may worthily receive, understand and live Thy Holy Gospel, through Christ our Lord. Amen.

GOSPEL

Stand for the Gospel. After the Gospel, Christ-priest gives a sermon. At this part of his Mass, he acts as Christ to his flock.

CREDO

Before beginning Mass, Christ-priest renews that profession of faith which defines us as Catholics:

CREDO in unum Deum, Patrem omnipotentem, factorem coeli et terrae, visibilium omnium et invisibilium. Et in unum Dominum Jesum Christum, Filium Dei unigenitum. Et ex Patre natum, ante omnia saecula. Deum de Deo, lumen de lumine, Deum verum de Deo vero. Genitum, non factum, consubstantialem Patri: per quem omnia facta sunt. Qui propter nos homines et propter nostram salutem descendit de coelis. (Genuflect) et incarnatus est de Spiritu Sancto ex Maria Virgine: ET HOMO FACTUS EST. (Rise) Crucifixus etiam pro nobis; sub Pontio Pilato passus, et sepultus est. Et resurrexit tertia die, secundum Scripturas. Et ascendit in coelum: sedet ad dexteram Patris. Et iterum venturus est cum gloria judicare vivos et mortuos: cujus regni non erit finis. Et in Spiritum Sanctum, Dominum et vivificantem: qui ex Patre, Filioque procedit. Qui cum Patre, et Filio simul adoratur, et conglorificatur: qui locutus est per Prophetas. Et unam, sanctam, Catholicam et Apostolicam Ecclesiam. Confiteor unum baptisma in remissionem peccatorum. Et exspecto resurrectionem mortuorum ✠ et vitam venturi saeculi. Amen.

CREED

I BELIEVE in one God, the Father Almighty, Creator of heaven and earth, and in all things visible and invisible. And in one Lord Jesus Christ, the Only begotten Son of God. Born of the Father before all ages. God of God; Light of Light; true God of true God. Begotten not made; of one being with the Father; by Whom all things were made. Who for us men, and for our salvation, came down from heaven. (Genuflect) And was made Flesh by the Holy Ghost of the Virgin Mary: AND WAS MADE MAN. (Rise) He was also crucified for us, suffered under Pontius Pilate and was buried. And on the third day He rose again according to the Scriptures. And ascending into heaven, He sits at the right hand of the Father. And He shall come again in glory to judge the living and the dead; and of His kingdom there shall be no end. And I believe in the Holy Ghost, the Lord and Giver of Life, Who proceeds from the Father and the Son, Who together with the Father and the Son is adored and glorified: Who spoke by the prophets. And I believe in one, holy, Catholic and Apostolic Church. I confess one baptism for the remission of sins. And I await the resurrection of the dead ✠ and the life of the world to come. Amen.

MASS OF THE FAITHFUL

MASS OF THE FAITHFUL

At each valid Mass, the Priest *in persona Christi,* as Christ, offers Christ. The Offerer and the Offered renews His effective Saving Will.

Through His anointed Christ-priest, Christ renews or redoes His Salutary Will. Through the powerful action of the Holy Spirit, the Holy Supper Sacrifice and Christ Himself, truly, mystically and sacramentally come into being.

Christ-priest defines his intention. Christ-priest *does not offer bread and wine.* As he prepares, he prays: I will offer–I will oblate--the Immaculate Victim–Christ.

The Mass is primarily the Salutary Oblation: "Christ's Oblation" in itself; and (as regards the Elect) "the Elect's oblation into Christ and His Oblation." Christ-priest offers "immaculatam hostiam."

SUSCIPE SANCTE PATER

Dominus vobiscum.

S. Et cum spiritu tuo.

Oremus.

SUSCIPE SANCTE PATER, omnipotens aeterne Deus, hanc immaculatam hostiam, quam ego indignus famulus tuus offero tibi Deo meo vivo et vero, pro innumerabilibus peccatis, et offensionibus, et negligentiis meis, et pro omnibus circumstantibus, sed et pro omnibus fidelibus christianis vivis atque defunctis: ut mihim et illis proficiat ad salutem in vitam aeternam. Amen.

The Mass is primarily the Salutary Oblation: "Christ's Oblation" in itself; and (as regards the Elect) "the Elect's oblation into Christ and His Oblation."

SUSCIPE SANCTE PATER

Christ-priest prays, offering the Immaculate Victim for our sins.

I OFFER "hanc immaculatam hostiam," the Immaculate Victim Christ and His Salutary Oblation (for sins). Thereby, I will realize God's Saving Will on earth as it is in Heaven. I, Christ-priest, will say Mass.

DEUS QUI

Christ-priest purposes to mystically/sacramentally oblate Christ, in order to unite the "life-oblations of the properly disposed" to Christ's Oblation, as symbolized by the drop of water being "taken into the wine" without changing the wine into water. So also do the Elect unite with Christ.

DEUS ✠ *qui humanae substantiae dignitatem mirabiliter condidisti, et mirabilius reformasti: da nobis per hujus aquae et vini mysterium, ejus divinitatis esse consortes, qui humanitatis nostrae fieri dignatus est particeps, Jesus Christus Filius tuus Dominus noster: Qui tecum vivit et regnat in unitate Spiritus Sancti Deus: per omnia saecula saeculorum. Amen.*

DEUS QUI

Christ-priest purposes to mystically/sacramentally oblate Christ, in order to unite the "life-oblations of the properly disposed" to Christ's Oblation, as symbolized by the drop of water being "taken into the wine" without changing the wine into water. So also do the Elect unite with Christ.

O GOD ✠ Who established the nature of man in wondrous dignity and still more admirably restored it, grant that by the Mystery of this water and wine, we may be made partakers of His Divinity (consortes) **Who deigned to partake of our humanity** (particeps) **Jesus Christ, Thy Son our Lord: Who with Thee lives and reigns in the unity of the Holy Ghost God, world without end. Amen.**

OFFERIMUS

 Christ-priest offers. In our hearts, we purpose (or "volitionally realize") our salutary oblations. We resolve to be united to or to become part of Christ's Salutary Oblation as expressed by "the Chalice of Salutary Sufferings."

OFFERIMUS tibi, Domine, calicem salutaris, tuam deprecantes clementiam: ut in conspectu divinae majestatis tuae, pro nostra et totius mundi salute cum odore suavitatis ascendat. Amen.

OFFERIMUS

Through Christ-priest, we offer: in our hearts. We purpose (or "volitionally realize") our salutary oblations. We resolve to be united to or to become part of Christ's Salutary Oblation as expressed by "the Chalice of Salutary Sufferings."

WE OFFER to Thee, O Lord, the Chalice of Salvation seeking Thy loving mercy that it may benefit us and others unto salvation from Hell. Amen.

In union with Thy Christ-priest as he offers *calicem salutaris,* I offer myself to Thee–through, with and in Christ our Lord. If Christ lives in me, it is to suffer and die. I offer Thee the Christ-chalice of my life–my chalice of salutary sufferings. Thus do I participate in Mass. Thus do I live the Mass.

IN SPIRITU HUMILITATIS

Making the Sign of the Cross with the chalice and placing it on the corporal, Christ-priest covers it with the pall.

IN SPIRITUS HUMILITATIS, et in animo contrito suscipiamur a te, Domine: et sic fiat sacrificium nostrum in conspectu tuo hodie, ut placeat tibi, Domine Deus.

VENI SANCTIFICATOR

Christ-priest "invokes" the Holy Spirit to mystically/sacramentally make present Christ's Oblation, (Holy Supper Sacrifice) and thus, Christ, Holy Sacrament; and, to take our life oblations into Christ's Oblation; and, thereby, (as members of Christ's Mystical Body) unto union with Christ-glorified (in Holy Sacrament). "Ut (in) nobis fiat corpus et sanquis dilectissimi Filii Tui" (*Quam Oblationem* prayers).

VENI, SANCTIFICATOR, omnipotens, aeterne Deus: et bene ✠ *dic hoc sacrificium tuo sancto nomini praeparatum.*

IN SPIRITU HUMILITATIS

May our life oblations be made *in spiritu humilitatis et in animo contrito* (humbly and sincerely) "into Christ-crucified" and, thereby, unto eternal joy in Heaven.

VENI SANCTIFICATOR

Christ-priest "invokes" the Holy Spirit to mystically/sacramentally make present Christ's

Oblation, (Holy Supper Sacrifice) and thus, Christ, Holy Sacrament; and, to take our life oblations into Christ's Oblation; and, thereby, (as members of Christ's Mystical Body) unto union with Christ-glorified (in Holy Sacrament). "Ut (in) nobis fiat corpus et sanquis dilectissimi Filii Tui" (*Quam Oblationem* prayers).

COME, HOLY GHOST, Almighty Eternal God, and bless ✠ this Sacrifice prepared in Thy name.

LAVABO Ps. 25:6-12

*LAVABO inter innocentes manus meas; et
circumdabo altare tuum, Domine.*

*Ut audiam vocem laudis: et enarrem
universa mirabilia tua.*

*Domine, dilexi decorem domus tuae:
et locum habitationis gloriae tuae.*

*Ne perdas cum impiis, Deus animam meam: et cum
viris sanguinum vitam meam.*

*In quorum manibus iniquitates sunt: dextera eorum
repleta est muneribus.*

*Ego autem in innocentia mea ingressus sum: redime
me, et miserere mei.*

*Pes meus stetit in directo: in ecclesiis benedicam te,
Domine.*

Gloria Patri et Filio et Spiritui Sancto.

*Sicut erat in principio, et nunc, et semper, et in
saecula saeculorum. Amen.*

LAVABO

Christ-priest prays:

As I (Christ-priest) wash my hands, I go around or encompass Christ the Altar. I resolve to re-do *(enarrem)* **what I have "heard"** *(audiam)***: Christ's Salutary Oblation, to bring the Holy Supper Sacrifice into mystical/sacramental being by my God-empowered speaking** *(dicens)* **at the Consecration of this Mass. O God, help me. Save me from priestly infidelity.**

Glory be to the Father and to the Son and to the Holy Ghost, as it was in the beginning, is now and ever shall be, world without end. Amen.

Prepare to offer yourself in sacrifice with Christ's Oblation as it comes to us through the action of the Christ-priest:

O Lord, I submit myself to Thee, through, with and in Thy saving Oblation.

SUSCIPE

Christ-priest prays that this Mass be accepted by the Blessed Trinity as Christ's Salutary Oblation so as to save us from Hell.

SUSCIPE SANCTA TRINITAS, hanc oblationem, quam tibi offerimus ob memoriam passionis,

resurrectionis, et ascensionis Jesu Christi Domini nostri: et in honorem beatae Mariae semper Virginis et beati Joannis Baptistae, et sanctorum Apostolorum Petri et Pauli, et istorum. Et omnium Sanctorum: ut illis proficiat ad honorem, nobis autem ad salutem: et illi pro nobis intercedere dignentur in coelis, quorum memoriam agimus in terris. Per eumdem Christum Dominum nostrum. Amen.

ORATE FRATRES

ORATE FRATRES, ut meum ac vestrum sacrificium acceptabile fiat apud Deum Patrem omnipotentem.

S. Suscipiat Dominus sacrificium de manibus tuis ad laudem, et gloriam nominis sui, ad utilitatem quoque nostram, totiusque Ecclesiae suae sanctae. Amen.

SUSCIPE SANCTA TRINITAS

ACCEPT, Most Holy Trinity, the oblation offered up to Thee in memory of the passion, resurrection and ascension of Jesus Christ our Lord; and in honor of Blessed Mary ever Virgin, Blessed John the Baptist, the Holy Apostles Peter and Paul, and all the saints that it may avail to their honor and aid our salvation; may they intercede in heaven for us who honor their memory here on earth.

ORATE FRATRES

PRAY, brethren, that our sacrifices, our oblations, ("in will and in deed") be accepted by God unto our eternal salvation.

Most Holy Trinity, accept my life-oblations through the Christ-oblation into the Memory of the passion, resurrection and ascension of Jesus. Save me from the Hell I deserve through Christ our Saviour.

PREFACE AND SANCTUS

These Preface prayers remind us that through Christ-priest's valid Mass, we enter into Christ's Eternal Oblation, Heaven's Mass.

Dominus vobiscum. S. Et cum spiritu tuo. P. Sursum corda. S. Habemus ad Dominum. P. Gratias agamus Domino Deo nostro. S. Dignum et justum est.

VERE dignum et justum est, aequum et salutare, nos tibi semper, et ubique gratias agere: Domine sancte, Pater omnipotens, aeterne Deus: Qui cum unigenito Filio tuo, et Spiritu Sancto, unus es Deus, unus es Dominus: non in unius singularitate personae, sed in unius Trinitate substantiae. Quod enim de tua gloria, revelante te, credimus, hoc de Filio tuo, hoc de Spiritu Sancto, sine differentia discretionis sentimus. Ut in confessione verae sempiternaeque Deitatis, et in personis proprietas, et in essentia unitas, et in majestate adoretur aequalitas. Quam laudant Angeli atque Archangeli, Cherubim quoque ac Seraphim: qui non cessant clamare quotidie, una voce dicentes: (Bell rings 3 times)

SANCTUS, SANCTUS, SANCTUS, Dominus Deus Sabaoth. Pleni sunt coeli et terra gloria tua. Hosanna in excelsis. ✠ Benedictus qui venit in nomine Domini. Hosanna in excelsis.

PREFACE AND SANCTUS

These prayers remind us that through Christ-priest's valid Mass, we enter into Christ's Eternal Oblation, Heaven's Mass.

HOSANNA! Save us! Thy Saving Oblation is about to materialize in our midst. Out of Thy Holy Sacrifice will come Thy Holy Sacrament.

Father, as Thou created, now Thou **blesseth. Bless into being the Eternal Oblation, Heaven: the soon to be present Lamb once slain and those of us, the Elect, who have been or will be, oblated through, with and in the Lamb, Jesus Christ.**

HOLY, HOLY, HOLY, Lord God Almighty! Heaven and earth are full of Thy glory! Hosanna in the highest!

TE IGITUR

TE IGITUR, clementissime Pater, per Jesum Christum Filium tuum Dominum nostrum, supplices rogamus ac petimus, (he kisses the altar) uti accepta habeas, et benedicas, haec ✠ dona, haec ✠ munera, haec ✠ sancta sacrificia illibata, in primis, quae tibi offerimus pro Ecclesia tua sancta catholica: quam pacificare, custodire, adunare, et regere digneris toto orbe terrarum:

una cum famulo tuo Papa nostro N., et Antistite nostro N., et omnibus orthodoxis, atque catholicae, et apostolicae fidei cultoribus.

TE IGITUR

We beseech Thee, most merciful and loving heavenly Father, through Thy Christ-priest, to accept and divinely metamorphosize (bless or salutarily oblate) both ourselves and this bread and wine. Save and sanctify sinful Catholics, especially, sinful, truly believing clergymen.

Through Christ-priest, we pray that "haec dona" (our "God givens") and "haec munera" (our accomplishments) may become "sancta sacrificia illibata" (God-pleasing oblations) through, with and in Christ. May the Holy Ghost sanctify us unto the glory of God the Father, now and forever and ever.

MEMENTO

As Christ-priest prays the intention for which the Mass is offered, mention here names of the persons and intentions for which you offer your Mass prayers to the Divine Victim.

MEMENTO, Domine, famulorum famularumque tuarum N. et N., et omnium circumstantium, quorum tibi fides cognita est, et nota devotio, pro quibus tibi offerimus: vel qui tibi offerunt hoc sacrificium laudis, pro se, suisque omnibus: pro redemptione animarum suarum, pro spe salutis, et incolumitatis suae: tibique reddunt vota sua aeterno Deo, vivo et vero.

COMMUNICANTES

Communicantes, et memoriam venerantes in primis gloriosae semper Virginis Marieae, Genitricis Dei et Domini nostri Jesu Christi: sed et beatorum Apostolorum ac Martyrum tuorum, Petri et Pauli, Andreae, Jacobi, Joannis, Thomae, Jacobi, Philippi, Bartholomaei, Matthaei, Simonis, et Thaddaei: Lini, Cleti, Clementis, Xysti, Cornelii, Cypriani, Laurentii Chrysogoni, Joannis et Pauli, Cosmae et Damiani: et omnium Sanctorum tuorum; quorum meritis precibusque concedas, ut in omnibus protectionis tuae muniamur auxilio. Per eumdem Christum Dominum nostrum. Amen.

MEMENTO   Commemoration of the Living

As Christ-priest prays the intention for which the Mass is offered, mention here names of the persons and intentions for which you offer your Mass prayers to the Divine Victim.

O Lord, make into Thy Eternal Memory (sacrificially oblate) unto fullness of joy, our life-oblations and the life-oblations of those for whom we pray.

COMMEMORATION of the Saints

Venerating the memories (lives) of the saints and desiring to be united with them–the glorious ever Virgin Mary, Mother of God and our Lord, Jesus Christ; the blessed Apostles and Martyrs, Peter and Paul, Andrew, James, John, Thomas, James, Philip, Bartholomew, Matthew, Simon and Thaddeus, Linus, Cletus, Clement, Sixtus, Cornelius, Cyprian, Lawrence, Chrysogonus, John and Paul, Cosmas and Damien, and all Thy saints–grant, O Lord, for the sake of their merits and prayers that in all thngs we may be guarded and helped by their intercessions on our behalf. Through the same Jesus Christ Our Lord. Amen.

HANC IGITUR

Bell is rung once.

For over a millenium, God's Old Testament priests placed their hands over each sacrificial victim. We are challenged to be so sacrificed. This prayer plus the Quam O b l a t i o n e m emphasize your oblation into the Christ-oblation.

HANC IGITUR oblationem servitutis nostrae, sed et cunctae familiae tuae, quaesumus, Domine, ut placatus accipias: diesque nostros in tua pace disponas, atque ab aeterna damnatione nos eripi, et in electorum tuorum jubeas grege numerari:
per Christum Dominum nostrum. Amen.

HANC IGITUR   *Bell is rung once.*

For over a millenium, God's Old Testament priests placed their hands over each sacrificial victim. We are challenged to be so sacrificed. This prayer plus the Quam Oblationem emphasize your oblation into the Christ-oblation.

May our life-oblations be conformed to Christ so as to please Thee, O God, now and forever. Keep us, O God, in Thy peace freed from sin and united to Thee; save us from Hell.

QUAM OBLATIONEM

Inasmuch as I become sanctified or oblated in and into Christ, Christ comes to be in me. The Holy Sacrifice produces the Holy Sacrament, at Mass and in me, now and forever. We can sense a certain urgency. Christ is coming! Only one whose life-oblation has been blessed into and united with Christ-oblation will lovingly commune with Christ both in time and in eternity.

Christ-priest recites the Quam Oblationem prayer, making the Sign of the Cross three times over the "host and chalice" together, once over the "host," and once over the "chalice" separately.

✠   ✠   ✠   ✠   ✠

Quam oblationem tu Deus, in omnibus quaesumus bene ✠ *dictam, adscrip* ✠ *tam, ra* ✠ *tam, rationabilem, acceptabilemque facere digneris: ut nobis Cor* ✠ *pus et San* ✠ *guis fiat dilectissimi Filii tui Domini nostri Jesu Christi.*

QUAM OBLATIONEM

Inasmuch as I become sanctified or oblated in and into Christ, Christ comes to be in me. The Holy Sacrifice produces the Holy Sacrament, at Mass and in me, now and forever. We can sense a certain urgency. Christ is coming! Only one whose life-oblation has been blessed into and united with Christ-oblation will lovingly commune with Christ both in time and in eternity.

    ✠   ✠   ✠   ✠   ✠

Deign, Heavenly Father, to oblate (salutarily bless) us "into Christ" and His Oblation (quam oblationem). Only thus will we become acceptable and pleasing to Thee (rationabilem acceptabilemque). By Thy grace, may Christ's Oblation be volitionally realized in our hearts ✠ (ratam-vowed) and vitally actualized in our deeds ✠ (adscriptam-accomplished). May we be so blessed ✠ (benedictam) that there comes to dwell in us (as members of Christ's Mystical Body) the Body and Blood ✠ of Thy dearly beloved Son, Our Lord, Jesus Christ. Amen.

Preface to the Consecration

Christ-priest has prayed that Christ's Oblation "Quam Oblationem" be in all of us. Now, in a mystical/sacramental manner, this Oblation (quam) will be "suffered into being" through Christ-priest *ex officio* "doing" *in persona Christi*, the Holy Supper Sacrifice. At this most solemn moment of Mass, oblate or dedicate yourself (as signing your earthly life) to be "likewise and thuswise" broken into Christ-crucified, unto being eternally united with Christ-glorified.

QUI PRIDIE

Qui pridie quam pateretur, accepit panem in sanctas, ac venerabiles manus suas, et elevatis oculis in coelum ad te Deum Patrem suum omnipotentem, tibi gratias agens, bene ✠ dixit, fregit, deditque discipulis suis, dicens:

Accipite, et manducate ex hoc omnes:

Hoc est enim Corpus meum.

Preface to the Consecration

Christ-priest has prayed that Christ's Oblation "Quam Oblationem" be in all of us. Now, in a mystical/sacramental manner, this Oblation (quam) will be "suffered into being" through Christ-priest *ex officio* "doing" *in persona Christi,* the Holy Supper Sacrifice. At this solemn moment of Mass, volitionally oblate yourself (as signing your earthly life) into Christ-crucified, unto being eternally united with Christ-glorified.

QUI PRIDIE

WHO, at the beginning of the day (Good Friday) on which He suffered the Oblation into being, He took bread into His holy and venerable hands, having lifted up His

eyes to Heaven to Thee, His almighty Father, giving thanks to Thee, blessed ✠ broke and gave to His disciples saying: All of you eat of Hoc:

for Hoc is my Body.

SIMILI MODO

Christ-priest pronounces the words of Consecration over the wine:

SIMILI MODO postquam coenatum est, accipiens et hunc praeclarum Calicem in sanctas ac venerabiles manus suas: item tibi gratias agens, bene ✠ dixit, deditque discipulis suis, dicens;

Accipite, et bibite ex eo omnes:

Hic est enim Calix Sanguinis mei, novi et aeterni testamenti, mysterium fidei, qui pro vobis et pro multis effundetur in remissionem peccatorum.

SIMILI MODO

The Holy Salutary Supper Sacrifice is mystically/sacramentally realized as Christ-priest presents and re-does what Christ did: Christ's Body, mystically/sacramentally broken "in and as" Sacrifice for sins so that His redeeming Blood may be shed for the salvation and sanctification of the Elect. Holy Sacrifice has "produced" Holy Sacrament.

Likewise, the sacrificial salutary oblations of our lives in, through and into Christ's Sacrifice or Oblation will accomplish our becoming the Mystical Body of Christ—our being united to Christ, Holy Sacrament, now and for all eternity. Offer and consecrate your body, mind and heart to be broken of self-love and "spent" in love of Christ unto the shedding of your blood.

Here, O Lord, is my body broken for Thee! Here, O Lord, is my blood, my life-force spent in service of Thee!

HAEC QUOTIESCUMQUE

Immediately after the Consecration of the wine, Christ-priest says in a low voice:

Haec quotiescumque feceritis, in mei memoriam facietis.

He kneels, adores the Sacred Victim and rises, elevating the Chalice of Salvation.

HAEC QUOTIESCUMQUE

As often as you (Christ-priest) do this, [Mass Oblation or Offering] there is "doing into My Memory."

Christ-priest completes the Salutary Supper Sacrifice as the shedding of Christ's Saving Blood is mystically/sacramentally repeated so that the Elect may be taken into His Memory:

As often as there is a "Mass-doing" here on earth, there is a "doing (faciens) into (Christ's) Eternal Memory."

The Mass does not merely recall a fait accompli. Mass "brings into being beneficiaries of Christ's Salutary Oblation." Mass brings into being "eternal memories" (as used in Eastern Liturgies) or "beneficiaries" (of "Memento") as used in the Canonized Latin Mass Liturgy.

✝

UNDE ET MEMORES

And thus (unde et) by reason of the Consecration, do Memores (eternal "partakers of the Memory") come into being; are sustained in being; and "are purposed in their eternal being."

UNDE ET MEMORES, Domine, nos servi tui, sed et plebs tua sancta, ejusdem Christi Filii tui Domini nostri tam beatae Passionis, nec non et ab inferis Resurrectionis, sed et in coelos gloriosaeAscensionis: offerimus praeclarae majestati tuae de tuis donis, ac datis, hostiam ✠ puram, hostiam ✠ sanctam, hostiam ✠ immaculatam, Panem ✠ sanctum vitae aeterne, et calicem ✠ salutis perpetuae.

UNDE ET MEMORES

THUS, through the mystery of faith done into the Memory, are we, Thy abject slaves, saved from Hell (unde) **and made into memores of Thy Son, Jesus Christ our Lord. We, Thy holy people, are taken into Christ's passion, His resurrection from the realm of death; and into His glorious ascension into Heaven. We offer to Thy Divine Majesty (of, from and because of) the once given and the continually being given: the pure Victim; the sanctifying ✠ Victim; the sin-conquering ✠ Victim—the Holy ✠ Bread: the Source, Sustenance and Summit of eternal life and the Chalice ✠ of our perpetually being saved from Hell and unto Heaven.**

SUPRA QUAE

Extending his hands, Christ-priest proceeds:

Supra quae propitio ac sereno vultu respicere digneris: et accepta habere, sicuti accepta habere dignatus es munera pueri tui justi Abel, et sacrificium patriarchae nostri Abrahae: et quod tibi obtulit summus sacerdos tuus Melchisedech, sanctum sacrificium, immaculatam hostiam.

SUPRA QUAE

Extending his hands, Christ-priest proceeds:

Now, O God, mercifully deign to accept our presently vowed life-oblations as Thou accepted those of Abel, Abraham and Melchisedech--through Christ and His Oblation.

SUPPLICES

Christ-priest bows and prays:

Supplices te rogamus, omnipotens Deus, jube haec perferri per manus sancti Angeli tui in sublime altare tuum, in conspectu divinae majestatis tuae; ut quotquot (he kisses the altar) *ex hac altaris, participatione sacrosanctum Filii tui Cor ✠ pus, et San ✠ guinem sumpserimus, omni benedictione coelesti et gratia repleamur. Per eumdem Christum Dominum nostrum. Amen.*

SUPPLICES

With greatest humility, fear and reverence, we beg Thee, Almighty God, that *haec oblationes*–the offerings or oblations of the faithful (Thy quotquot) may somehow be taken by Thy Holy Angel into the sight of Thy Divine Majesty, to Thine altar on High so that we who dare to receive the Body ✠ and Blood ✠ of Christ Thy Son, may be filled with graces and blessings from Heaven, through Christ, Our Lord. Amen.

MEMENTO

Memento etiam, Domine, famulorum famularumque tuarum N. et N., qui nos praecesserunt cum signo fidei, et dormiunt in somno pacis. Ipsis, Domine, et omnibus in Christo quiescentibus, locum refrigerii lucis et pacis ut indulgeas, deprecamur:

per eumdem Christum Dominum nostrum. Amen.

†

MEMENTO

**May this Mass,
C h r i s t ' s
Oblation, the
S u p p e r
Sacrifice, help
b r i n g   t h e
departed souls of
....** (name the
departed souls for
whom you wish to
pray) **into full
enjoyment of the
Beatific Vision.**

†

NOBIS QUOQUE PECCATORIBUS

NOBIS QUOQUE PECCATORIBUS famulis tuis, de multitudine miserationum tuarum sperantibus, partem aliquam, et societatem donare digneris, cum tuis sanctis Apostolis et Martyribus: cum Joanne, Stephano, Matthia, Barnaba, Ignatio, Alexandro, Marcellino, Petro, Felicitate, Perpetua, Agatha, Lucia, Agnete, Caecilia, Anastasia, et omnibus Sanctis tuis: intra quorum nos consortium, non aestimator meriti, sed veniae, quasumus, largitor admitte. Per Christum Dominum nostrum.

NOBIS QUOQUE PECCATORIBUS

Grant, O Lord, to us sinners, a place with Thy holy Apostles and Martyrs:

John
Stephen
Matthias
Barnabas
Ignatius
Alexander
Marcellinus
Peter
Felicitas
Perpetua
Agatha
Lucy
Agnes
Cecilia
Anastasia
and all Thy saints.

Look not upon our merits, nor upon what we deserve, but in Thy great mercy, pardon us our sins, through Jesus Christ, our Lord.

PER QUEM...PER IPSUM

As we purpose to be salutarily oblated in, into and through Christ and His Oblation, we remember that we are sinners by birth and inclination; as well as, in deed and habit. We pray for God's mercy and loving-kindness in our regard.

Per quem haec omnia, Domine, semper bona creas, sancti ✠ ficas vivi ✠ ficas bene ✠ dicis et praestas nobis.

Per ip ✠ sum, et cum ip ✠ so, et in ip ✠ so, est tibi Deo Patri ✠ omnipotenti, in unitate Spiritus ✠ Sancti, omnis honor et gloria.

P. Per omnia saecula saeculorum.

S. Amen.

PER QUEM...PER IPSUM

As we purpose to be salutarily oblated in, into and through Christ and His Oblation, we remember that we are sinners by birth and inclination; in deed and habit. We pray for God's loving-kindness. Through Christ, God gives to the Elect. Through Christ, the Elect fittingly respond to God.

Through Christ our Lord, do Thou, Heavenly Father and Holy Ghost, create ✠ and provide; transform ✠ and sanctify ✠ Thine Elect and that which Thou dost graciously bestow upon them.

Through ✠ Him (Christ and His Salutary Supper Sacrifice); with ✠ Him and in ✠ Him, is to Thee, God, Father ✠ Almighty, in union with the Holy ✠ Ghost, all honor and glory, world without end. Amen.

These two Christological prayers summarily conclude the "more strictly binding" Canonized Latin Mass Prayers.

PATER NOSTER

Preface to Holy Communion

On behalf of the faithful, Christ-priest now prays for Christ's peace *(pax divina vivens)* through Holy Communion.

P. Oremus. Praeceptis salutaribus moniti, et divina institutione formati, audemus dicere:

PATER NOSTER, qui es in coelis; sanctificetur nomen tuum: adveniat regnum tuum: fiat voluntas tua, sicut in coelo, et in terra. Panem nostrum quotidianum da nobis hodie: et dimitte nobis debita nostra, sicut et nos dimittimus debitoribus nostris. Et ne nos inducas in tentationem.

S.   Sed libera nos a malo.   P.Amen.

In this life, Christ's peace is freedom from sin and a life lived in Sanctifying Grace; in eternity, Christ's peace is freedom from Hell plus enjoyment of the eternally ecstatic vision of God.

OUR FATHER

May Thy Masses be done on earth as in Heaven: "Thy (salutary) Will be done on earth as it is in Heaven."

OUR FATHER, who art in heaven. Hallowed be Thy name. Thy kingdom come. Thy Will be done; on earth as it is in heaven.

Give us this day our daily bread. And forgive us our trespasses as we forgive those who trespass against us.

Lead us not into temptation, but deliver us from evil. Amen.

"Lead us not yield to sin; deliver us from evil." We pray for peace: freedom from sin and Hell; and, union with Christ.

LIBERA NOS

The Consecration gave us Christ's broken Body and His shed Blood. The Consecration gave us the Salutary Oblation into which we "re-vowed" our lives.

On our behalf, Christ-priest prays for pax divina vivens–freedom from sin and its effects and ever greater union with Christ.

Christ-priest takes the paten between the first and second finger and says:

LIBERA NOS, quaesumus, Domine, ab omnibus malis, praeteritis praesentibus, et futuris: et intercedente beata, et gloriosa semper Virgine Dei Genitrice Maria cum beatis Apostolis tuis Petro et Paulo, atque Andrea, et omnibus Sanctis, (Christ-priest signs himself with the paten and kisses it) da propitius pacem in diebus nostris: ut ope misericordiae tuae adjuti, et a peccato simus semper liberi, et ab omni perturbatione securi.

LIBERA NOS

Now, Holy Sacrifice "in Holy Sacrament" anticipates Heaven. The Mass Liturgy provides the faithful with "foretaste and promise" of eternally "ecstatic victory" – union or Holy Communion with Christ-glorified.

Christ-priest takes the paten between the first and second finger and says:

DELIVER US, we beseech Thee, O Lord, from all evils, past, present and to come. And by the intercession of the Blessed and glorious ever Virgin Mary, Mother of God, and of all Thy saints, ✠ mercifully grant peace in our days, that through Thy loving mercy, we may be always free from sin and its effects.

Sanctify us. Purge us from sin. Make us worthy to commune with Christ, now and forever.

FRACTIO ET COMMIXTIO

Concluding the Libera Nos, Christ-priest takes "Hoc" (the Sacred Host), breaks It in the middle over the Chalice, saying:

Per eumdem Dominum nostrum Jesum Christum Filium tuum.

(He breaks off a Particle from the divided "Hoc":)

Qui tecum vivit et regnat in unitate Spiritus Sancti Deus. Per omnia saecula saeculorum. S. Amen.

Christ-priest makes the Sign of the Cross with the Particle over the Chalice, saying:

Pax ✠ Domini, sit ✠ semper vobis ✠ cum.

S. Et cum spiritu tuo.

Christ-priest puts the Particle into the Chalice, saying:
Haec commixtio, et consecratio Corporis et Sanguinis Domini nostri Jesu Christi, fiat accipientibus nobis in vitam aeternam. Amen.

✠   ✠   ✠

FRACTIO ET COMMIXTIO

Concluding the Libera Nos, Christ-priest takes "Hoc" (the Sacred Host), breaks It in the middle over the Chalice, saying:

Through the same Jesus Christ Thy Son, our Lord (He breaks off a Particle from the divided "Hoc":) **Who lives and reigns with Thee in the unity of the Holy Ghost, God, world without end. Amen.**

Christ-priest makes the Sign of the Cross with the Particle over the Chalice, saying:

May the peace ✠ of the Lord ✠ be always with ✠ you.   S. And with thy spirit.

Christ-priest puts the Particle into the Chalice, saying:

May the Body and Blood of our Lord Jesus Christ bring those of us who receive Holy Communion unto eternal life in Heaven. Amen.

✠   ✠   ✠

Most Sacred Heart of Jesus,
Have mercy on us!

FRACTIO ET COMMIXTIO

In a mystical/ sacramental way, the consecration separated Christ's broken Body from His shed Blood. The consecration is Holy Sacrifice.

However, as Holy Sacrifice occurs, Holy Sacrament happens. Now the breaking of Hoc and the uniting of the sacred species "physically signs" Christ-glorified, Holy Sacrament.

"What" was effected by separate consecrations (Holy Sacrifice) is now "physically signed" as "union of sacred species" in Christ-glorified, Holy Sacrament." From this time on, the Mass prayers primarily address Christ-glorified.

✠ ✠ ✠

AGNUS DEI

Christ is Saviour. He saves from sin. Eternally, He is Lamb of God (cf. Apocalypse). He is Source, Sustenance and "Object" of peace, which is eternal life without Hell; and, temporal life without sin.

AGNUS DEI,
qui tollis peccata mundi;
miserere nobis.

AGNUS DEI,
qui tollis peccata mundi:
miserere nobis.

AGNUS DEI,
qui tollis peccata mundi:
dona nobis pacem.

AGNUS DEI

Christ is Saviour. He saves from sin. Eternally, He is Lamb of God (cf. Apocalypse). He is Source, Sustenance and "Object" of peace, which is eternal life without Hell; and, temporal life without sin.

LAMB OF GOD,
Who takest away the sins of the world, have mercy on us.

LAMB OF GOD,
Who takest away the sins of the world, have mercy on us.

LAMB OF GOD,
Who takest away the sins of the world, grant us peace.

PRIEST PREPARES FOR HOLY COMMUNION

Christ-priest prays the following prayers to our Lord
Jesus Christ, here before him in Holy Sacrament. He
prays for Christ's existential church and for himself.

DOMINE Jesu Christe, qui dixisti Apostolis tuis:
Pacem relinquo vobis, pacem meam do vobis: ne
respicias peccata mea, sed fidem Ecclesiae tuae:
eamque secundum voluntatem tuam pacificare et
coadunare digneris: Qui vivis et regnas Deus per
omnia saecula saeculorum. Amen.

DOMINE Jesu Christe, Fili Dei vivi qui ex voluntate
Patris, cooperante Spiritu Sancto, per mortem tuam
mundum vivificasti: libera me per hoc sacrosanctum
Corpus et Sanguinem tuum ab omnibus iniquitatibus
meis, et universis malis: et fac me tuis semper
inhaerere mandatis, et a te numquam separari
permittas: Qui cum eodem Deo Patre, et Spiritu
Sancto vivis et regnas Deus in saecula saeculorum.
Amen

PRIEST PREPARES FOR HOLY COMMUNION

In the first prayer, Christ-priest prays for Christ's Church on earth that it may cherish, provide and hand on intact--Holy Gifts, the Source, Sustenance and "Object" of Peace–the Canonized Mass. He prays for peace and unity according to God's Will. In the other prayers, he prays for himself.

O Lord Jesus Christ, Who didst say to Thine Apostles: Peace I leave you, My peace I give you: look not upon my sins, but upon the faith of Thy Church: and deign to give her that peace and unity which is agreeable to Thy Will: God Who lives and reigns, world without end. Amen.

Lord, Thou hast made Thy Holy Sacrifice our source of Peace (freedom from sin and communion with Thee). May my Holy Communion effect my life-oblation through, in and into Thee and Thy Salutary Oblation.

PRIEST PREPARES FOR HOLY COMMUNION

Perceptio Corporis tui, Domine Jesu Christe, quod ego indignus sumere praesumo, non mihi proveniat in judicium et condemnationem: sed pro tua pietate, prosit mihi ad tutamentum mentis et corporis, et ad medelam percipiendam. Qui vivis et regnas cum Deo Patre in unitate Spiritus Sancti Deus, per omnia saecula saeculorum, Amen.

PRIEST RECEIVES HOLY COMMUNION

Christ-priest genuflects, rises and says:

Panem caelestem accipiam, et nomen Domini invocabo.

Bell rings thrice.   Christ-priest says thrice:

Domine, non sum dignus, ut intres sub tectum meum: sed tantum dic verbo, et sanabitur anima mea.

Making the Sign of the Cross with the Sacred Sacrament over the paten, he says:

Corpus Domini nostri Jesu Christi custodiat animam meam in vitam aeternam. Amen.

PRIEST PREPARES for HOLYCOMMUNION

Let not my present Holy Communion be unto my eternal condemnation; but may it safeguard and strengthen me unto eternal Holy Communion with Thee, Lord Jesus Christ. Amen.

PRIEST RECEIVES HOLY COMMUNION

Christ-priest genuflects, rises and says:

I will take the Bread of Heaven and will call upon the name of the Lord.

Bell rings thrice. Christ-priest says thrice:

LORD, I am not worthy that Thou shouldst enter under my roof; but only say the word, and my soul will be healed.

Making the Sign of the Cross with the Sacred Sacrament over the paten, he says:

May the Body ✠ of our Lord Jesus Christ preserve my soul unto life everlasting. Amen.

PRIEST RECEIVES HOLY COMMUNION

Christ-priest receives both halves of the Sacrament. Uncovering the Chalice, he genuflects, collects whatever Fragments may remain on the corporal and purifies the paten over the Chalice, saying:

Quid retribuam Domino pro omnibus quae retribuit mihi? Calicem salutaris accipiam, et nomen Domini invocabo. Laudans invocabo Dominum, et ab inimicis meis salvus ero.

With the Chalice, he makes the Sign of the Cross, saying:

Sanguis Domini nostri Jesu Christi custodiat animam meam in vitam aeternam. Amen.

Then he receives the Precious Blood.

PRIEST RECEIVES HOLY COMMUNION

Christ-priest receives both halves of the Sacrament. Uncovering the Chalice, he genuflects, collects whatever Fragments may remain on the corporal and purifies the paten over the Chalice, saying:

What return shall I make to the Lord for all that He hath given me? I will take the chalice of salvation, and call upon the name of the Lord. I will call upon the Lord and praise Him in order to be saved from my enemies.

With the Chalice, he makes the Sign of the Cross, saying:

May the Blood ✠ of our Lord Jesus Christ preserve my soul unto life everlasting. Amen.

Then he receives the Precious Blood.

COMMUNION OF THE LAITY

The Confiteor is said. Then Christ-priest prays:

Misereatur vestri omnipotens Deus, et dimissis peccatis vestris, perducat vos ad vitam aeternam. S. Amen.

Making the Sign of the Cross, he continues:

Indulgentiam, ✠ *absolutionem, et remissionem peccatorum vestrorum tribuat vobis omnipotens, et misericors Dominus. S. Amen.*

[If laity are present and consider themselves "worthy to receive," there now follows the reception of Communion.] Elevating the Blessed Sacrament and turning toward the people, he says:

Ecce Agnus Dei, ecce qui tollit peccata mundi.

Then he says three times:

Domine, non sum dignus, ut intres sub tectum meum: sed tantum dic verbo, et sanabitur anima mea.

COMMUNION OF THE LAITY

The Confiteor is said. Then, Christ-priest prays:

May Almighty God have mercy on you, forgive you your sins, and bring you to life everlasting. Amen.

Making the Sign of the Cross, he continues:

May the almighty and merciful Lord grant you pardon, absolution and remission of your sins. Amen.

[If laity are present and consider themselves "worthy to receive," they do so now.] Elevating the Blessed Sacrament and turning toward the people, he says:

Behold, the Lamb of God, behold Him Who taketh away the sins of the world.

Then he says three times:

Lord, I am not worthy that Thou should enter under my roof, say but the word and my soul will be healed.

COMMUNION OF THE LAITY

He administers Communion (on the tongue) to the kneeling laity saying to each:

Corpus Domini nostri Jesu Christi custodiat animam tuam in vitam aeternam. Amen.

If you do not receive Communion at this Mass, make an act of Spiritual Communion.

Quod ore sumpsimus, Domine, pura mente capiamus: et de munere temporali fiat nobis remedium sempiternum.
Corpus tuum, Domine, quod sumpsi, et Sanguis, quem potavi, adhaereat visceribus meis: et praesta; ut in me non remaneat scelerum macula, quem pura et sancta refecerunt sacramenta: Qui vivis et regnas in saecula saeculorum. Amen.

COMMUNION OF THE LAITY

He administers Communion (on the tongue) to the kneeling faithful saying to each:

May the Body ✠ of our Lord Jesus Christ preserve your soul unto life everlasting. ("Eternal Memory" be yours.)

If you do not receive Communion at this Mass, make an act of Spiritual Communion.

Grant, O Lord, that what we have received with our mouth, we may assimilate with pure minds; and that this temporal gift may become for us an everlasting remedy and the eternal source of Beatific Life.

Christ-priest holds out the Chalice to the server who pours wine into it for the first ablution.

May Thy Body and Blood, O Lord, become part of my innermost being and grant that through this Holy Sacrifice and Holy Sacrament, no stain of sin remain in me. Who livest and reignest forever. Amen.

Christ-priest washes his fingers and receives the second ablution. He prays the Communion Proper and then, kisses the altar.

Dominus vobiscum. S. Et cum spiritu tuo.
Oremus.

Christ-priest prays the Postcommunion Proper.

Amen. Dominus vobiscum. S. Et cum spiritu tuo.

Ite, Missa est.   S. Deo gratias.

Ite, Missa Est

You have mystically (in this Mystery of Faith) been taken into Heaven, Christ's Eternal Oblation, to renew and have renewed within you the vow or promise of your own life-oblation in, into and through Christ and His Oblation (through Holy Sacrifice of the Mass).

If you have properly prayed the Mass, you have realized–made real for your life–God's Salutary Oblation through Christ. Now, you are to actualize Christ's Salutary Oblation. Now, go live the Mass.

Christ-priest washes his fingers and receives the second ablution. He prays the Communion Proper and then, kisses the altar.

P. The Lord be with you.   S. And also with you. Let us pray.

Christ-priest prays the Postcommunion Proper.

Amen.
The Lord be with you.   S. And also with you.
P. Go the Mass is ended. S. Thanks be to God.

Ite, Missa Est

Imitate Christ-crucified in His earthly life, climaxing in His Passion and Death. By grace, ever strive to have Christ's Saving Will or Christ's Salutary Oblation (His Sacrifice) actualized in your own life.

"Go, you are so sent! Go, that's your mission: to live the Mass! Ite missa est!"

THE LAST BLESSING

Placeat tibi, sancta Trinitas, obsequium servitutis meae: et praesta: ut sacrificium, quod oculis tuae majestatis indignus obtuli, tibi sit acceptabile, mihique et omnibus, pro quibus illud obtuli, sit, te miserante, propitiabile. Per Christum Dominum nostrum. Amen.

Turning to the faithful, Christ-priest invokes the Blessing of God, making the Sign of the Cross over them.

Benedicat vos omnipotens Deus, Pater, et Filius ✠ et Spiritus Sanctus. S. Amen.

Dominus vobiscum.   *S. Et cum spiritu tuo.*
Initium ✠ sancti Evangelii secundum Joannem.
S. Gloria tibi, Domine.

THE LAST BLESSING

May Christ's Salutary Oblation as "re-done or re-presented" by me, Christ-priest, please Thee, Almighty God.

Turning to the faithful, Christ-priest invokes the Blessing of God, making the Sign of the Cross over them.

May the Almighty God bless you: the Father and the Son ✠ and the Holy Ghost. Amen.

The Lord be with you. S. And with thy spirit. The beginning ✠ of the Holy Gospel of St. John.   S. Glory be to Thee, O Lord.

The Last Gospel

In principio erat Verbum, et Verbum erat apud Deum, et Deus erat Verbum. Hoc erat in principio apud Deum, Omnia per ipsum facta sunt: et sine ipso factum est nihil quod factum est: in ipso vita erat, et vita erat lux hominum: et lux in tenebris lucet, et tenebrae eam non comprehenderunt. Fuit homo missus a Deo, cui nomen erat Joannes. Hic venit in testimonium, ut testimonium perhiberet de lumine, ut omnes crederent per illum. Non erat ille lux, sed ut testimonium perhiberet de lumine. Erat lux vera quae illuminat omnem hominem venientem in hunc mundum. In mundo erat, et mundus per ipsum factus est et mundus eum non cognovit. In propria venit, et sui eum non receperunt. Quotquot autem receperunt eum, dedit eis potestatem filios Dei fieri, his, qui credunt in nomine ejus: qui non ex sanguinibus, neque ex voluntate carnis, neque ex voluntate viri, sed ex Deo nati sunt.   (Genuflect)

ET VERBUM CARO FACTUM EST, et habitavit in nobis: et vidimus gloriam ejus, gloriam quasi Unigeniti a Patre, plenum gratiae et veritatis.

S. Deo gratias.

THE LAST GOSPEL

In the beginning was the Word, and the Word was with God; and the Word was God. He was in the beginning with God. All things were made through Him, and without Him was made nothing that has been made. In Him was life, and the life was the light of men. And the light shines in the darkness; and the darkness grasped it not. There was a man, one sent from God, whose name was John. This man came as a witness, to bear witness concerning the Light, that all might believe through Him. He was not himself the light, but was to bear witness to the light. It was the true Light that enlightens every man who comes into the world. He was in the world, and the world knew Him not. He came unto His own, and His own received Him not. But to as many as received Him He gave the power of becoming sons of God; to those who believe in His Name: who were born not

St. Padre Pio, priest-saint of the Canonized Mass, help restore the Canonized Mass among us.

St. Padre Pio, pray for us!

of blood, nor of the will of the flesh, nor of the will of man, but of God.   (genuflect) AND THE WORD WAS MADE FLESH and dwelt among us. And we saw his glory, the glory as of the Only-begotten of the Father, full of grace and of truth. S. Thanks be to God.

God's Revelation, Christ Jesus, is rejected by most of mankind. *Quotquot,* however, receive Him and accept Him and, thereby, become Catholics in spirit and in truth.

However, to attain Heaven, *quotquot* must have the Saving Will "actualized into them" by being salutarily oblated in, into and through Christ the Way; living by grace as Christ and His Church demand but, not living in conformity to the desires of one's flesh; nor living "for or from" another human person. Only those who offer pure life-oblations in, into and through Christ and His Oblation will be birthed into *(nati sunt)* God and His ecstatic eternal life.

To be said after the celebration of Low Mass.

AVE MARIA (3 times)

AVE, MARIA, gratia plena; dominus tecum: benedicta tu in mulieribus, et benedictus fructus ventris tui Jesus.

SANCTA MARIA, Mater Dei, ora pro nobis peccatoribus, nunc et in hora mortis nostrae. Amen

SALVE REGINA

SALVE, REGINA, Mater misericordiae, vita, dulcedo, et spes nostra, salve. Ad te clamamus, exsules filii Hevae. Ad te suspiramus gementes et flentes in hac lacrymarum valle. Eia ergo, advocata nostra, illos tuos misericordes oculos ad nos converte. Et Jesum, benedictum fructum ventris tui, nobis, post hoc exsilium, ostende. O clemens, O pia, O dulcis Virgo Maria.

P. Ora pro nobis, sancta Dei Genitrix.
R. Ut digni efficiamur promissionibus Christi.

HAIL MARY (3 times)

HAIL MARY, full of grace. The Lord is with thee. Blessed art thou among women and blessed is the fruit of thy womb, Jesus.

HOLY MARY, Mother of God, pray for us sinners, now and at the hour of our death. Amen.

HAIL HOLY QUEEN

 HAIL, HOLY QUEEN, Mother of Mercy, our life, our sweetness and our hope! To thee do we cry, poor banished children of Eve; to thee do we send up our sighs, mourning and weeping in this valley of tears.

Turn then, most gracious advocate, thine eyes of mercy towards us; and after this our exile, show unto us the blessed fruit of thy womb, Jesus. O clement, O loving, O sweet Virgin Mary.

Pray for us, O holy Mother of God.
R. That we may be made worthy of the promises of Christ.

Oremus.

DEUS, refugium nostrum et virtus, populum ad te clamantem propitius respice; et intercedente gloriosa et Immaculata Virgine Dei Genitrice Maria, cum beato Joseph, ejus Sponso, ac beatis Apostolis tuis Petro et Paulo, et omnibus Sanctis, quas pro conversione peccatorum, pro libertate et exaltatione sanctae Matris Ecclesiae, preces effundimus, misericors et benignus exaudi. Per eumdem Christum Dominum nostrum.
R. Amen.

SANCTE MICHAEL ARCHANGELE, defende nos in proelio, contra nequitiam et insidias diaboli esto praesidium. Imperet illi Deus, supplices deprecamur: tuque, Princeps militiae caelestis, Satanam aliosque spiritus malignos, qui ad perditionem animarum pervagantur in mundo, divina virtute, in infernum detrude.

R. Amen. Cor Jesu sacratissimum,
R. Miserere nobis.

Let us pray.

O GOD, our refuge and our strength, look down in mercy on Thy people who cry to Thee; and by the intercession of the glorious and Immaculate Virgin Mary, Mother of God, of Saint Joseph her spouse, of Thy blessed Apostles Peter and Paul, and of all the Saints, in mercy and goodness, hear our prayers for the conversion of sinners, and for the liberty and exaltation of our holy mother, the Church, through the same Christ our Lord. Amen.

ST. MICHAEL the ARCHANGEL, defend us in battle; be our safeguard against the wickedness and snares of the devil. May God rebuke him, we humbly pray; and do Thou, O Prince of the heavenly hosts, by the power of God, cast into Hell, satan and all the evil spirits, who wander through the world seeking the ruin of souls. Amen.

P. Most Sacred Heart of Jesus, (3 times)
R. Have mercy on us.

SUSCIPE of ST. IGNATIUS LOYOLA

TAKE, O LORD, and receive my entire liberty, my memory, my understanding, and my whole will.

All that I am, and all that I possess, Thou hast given me: I surrender it all to Thee to be disposed of according to Thy Will.

Give me only Thy love and Thy grace; with these, I will be rich enough, and I desire nothing more.

ANIMA CHRISTI

**SOUL of CHRIST, sanctify me.
Body of Christ, save me.**

**Blood of Christ, give me life.
Water from the side of Christ, wash me.
Passion of Christ, strengthen me.**

**O Good Jesus, hear me.
Within Thy wounds, hide me.**

**Never permit me to be separated from
Thee.
From the malignant enemy, defend me.**

**At the hour of death, call me, and bid me
come to Thee, that with Thy saints, I may
praise Thee forever and ever.   Amen.**

"Agonize"

At Mass, you "volitionally realize" (or make) your salutary oblation. You purpose to be oblated into Christ-crucified unto Christ-glorified.

You make salutary "rata" (promise or vow). Now you need to "vitally actualize" your "purposed" salutary oblation. Not everyone who says, "Lord, Lord" (or who even purposes to follow the Lord) goes to Heaven; but, only he who actualizes his salutary oblation will go to Heaven (cf. Mt 7).

"Agonize" to actualize your Mass-enabled "volitionally realized" salutary oblation. By God's graces and your graced cooperation, make your "rata consumata.."

One must agonize to truly participate in

Mass or to make Mass into the prayer of one's life. "Agonize" is the English "cognate" of the original Greek biblical word "agonizethai."

Agonize to beat the odds, which are against you. Desire God. Desire only God! Live obsessed with God! Be spiritually a fanatic for God, by God's grace and your graced cooperation, realize and actualize God's Salutary Will, Christ's Oblation in your life:

> **He said unto them 'agonizethai' [agonize] to enter through the narrow gate; many will seek to enter but without sufficient determination.**
> **Lu 13:24**

Offering Mass Continually

The Victim is one and the same, the same now offering by the ministry of the priest [who operates in persona Christi] who once offered Himself on the cross, the manner of offering alone being different.

The dogmatic Council of Trent

Catholicism dogmatically teaches that the Mass is the Unbloody Salutary Sacrifice. At every canonized Mass, Christ offers and is (bloodlessly) sacrificed for the salvation and sanctification of sinners:

The August sacrifice of the altar is...a true and proper act of sacrifice, whereby the High Priest, by an unbloody immolation, offers Himself, as a most acceptable Victim to the Eternal Father, as He did upon the cross.

Mediator Dei, Pope Pius XII, 1947

To be salutarily beneficial to oneself, one must pray the canonized Mass as Christ's Salutary Oblation and as one's own salutary oblation into and through Christ's Oblation. Every canonized Mass is of "priceless worth" both "in itself" and for oneself. However, the Mass does not stop at the "Ite Missa est" (which means "Go, as being sent").

In this prayerbook, as we showed how to pray the canonized Mass as Salutary Offering, we also mentioned the ongoing continual need to "actualize" or execute Salutary Oblation: to pray the Mass "outside of Mass or to "live the Mass" in mind, heart and deed. Only by praying the Mass at Mass, as well as, "outside of Mass" by living the Mass daily, can one be saved and sanctified.

The Church dogmatically teaches "in theory and in practice" that the sacrament of

Baptism allows one to come to Mass, to come to the Unbloody Oblation. How can one escape eternal damnation if he fails to properly respond to God's "great Salutary Plan" (Heb 2:3) both at Mass and "outside of Mass?"

The Roman Catholic Church put great emphasis on fulfilling one's salutary obligations through its devotion to the "Morning Offering" and other like offerings during the day. Thereby, the dogmatically teaching Church showed us how to effectively and salutarily appropriate the Canonized Mass as our own "outside of Mass" as well as, at Mass.

Throughout the Day Renew the Salutary Oblation of the Holy Mass Sacrifice

During the last years of authentic Latin Rite Masses, the Morning Offering and like offerings became part of the daily life of every devout Catholic. Daily, each Catholic offered his own sufferings and joys of the day (in union with all the Masses being said throughout the world) for sinners–himself and others.

These "Mass offering prayers," were conducive to: (1) a greater appreciation of the Mass as Salutary Oblation (Christ's and our own); (2) renewing our salutary oblations (our Mass oblations); (3) helping us look forward to praying the next Mass; and, (4) bringing about the salvation and sanctification of souls.

Most Sacred Heart of Jesus,
have mercy on us!

Offering of Mass

Heavenly Father, Father of mercies, for love of us, Thou hast given Thy only begotten Son, Who sacrificed Himself upon the cross, and for our sake, doth continually renew that sacrifice of Himself upon our altars. And, therefore, do I–sinner, but penitent; poor, but rich in Jesus Christ–present myself before Thee. With the love of angels and of all Thy saints, and with the tender affection of the Immaculate Heart of Mary, I offer to Thee the Masses which are now being celebrated together with all those which have been celebrated, and which shall be celebrated to the end of the world.

Moreover, I intend to renew the offering of them every moment of this day and of all my life, that I may thereby render to Thy infinite majesty an honor and a glory worthy of Thee, thus to appease Thy indignation, to satisfy Thy justice for our many sins, to render Thee thanks in proportion to Thy benefits, and to implore Thy mercies for myself and for all sinners, for all the faithful, living and dead, for Thy whole Church, and principally, for its visible head, the Sovereign Pontiff, and lastly, for all poor schismatics, heretics, and infidels, that they also may be converted and save their souls.

Pope Pius IX, April 11, 1860
Indulgence of three years.

Another Offering of Mass

Eternal Father, I offer to Thee the Sacrifice which Thy beloved Son Jesus made of Himself upon the cross, and which He now renews upon this altar; I offer it to Thee together with the Masses which have been celebrated, and which shall be celebrated in the whole world. In order to adore Thee, and to give Thee the honor which Thou dost deserve, to render to Thee due thanks for Thy innumerable benefits, to appease Thy anger, which our many sins have provoked, and to give Thee due satisfaction for them, to entreat Thee also for myself, for the Church, for the whole world, and for the blessed souls in purgatory. Amen.

Indulgence-- 3 yrs.
Pope Pius IX, Apr. 11, 1860

Offering for Sinners
Who Are in Their Agony

My God, I offer Thee all the Masses that are celebrated throughout the world today, for sinners who are in their agony and who must die this day. May the Precious Blood of Jesus, the Redeemer, obtain mercy for them.

Pope Pius X, Dec. 18, 1907
Indulgence of 300 days

Fatima-Given Offering

The initial year of the God-given Fatima Message, Sr. Lucia gave us the famous "angel-bestowed offertory prayer."

Most Holy Trinity, Father, Son and Holy Spirit, I adore Thee profoundly.

I offer Thee the most precious Body, Blood, Soul and Divinity of Jesus Christ, present in all the tabernacles of the world, in reparation for the outrages, sacrileges and indifferences with which He Himself is offended.

Through the infinite merits of His most Sacred Heart and the Immaculate Heart of Mary, I beg of Thee, the conversion of poor sinners.

Angel Prayer at Fatima, 1916

The Morning Offering
and the
Holy Sacrifice of the Mass

In effect, the angel taught us to adore Holy Sacrament unto the conversion of sinners and in reparation to the Sacred Heart. This same sentiment is repeated in the classical Morning Offering.

O Jesus, through the Immaculate Heart of Mary, I offer Thee all my prayers, works, joys and sufferings of this day, for the intentions of Thy most Sacred Heart, in union with the celebration of the Holy Sacrifice of the Mass throughout the world, in reparation for my sins, for the conversion of sinners, for the good of the Church, for the Holy Father and the Holy Apostolic See.

TOLL FREE: 1-888-577-4428

www.maeta.com

MAETA   POB 6012   METAIRIE LA 70009-6012